IT'S A DIGITAL WORLD!

Master
Computer Programmers

Christine E. Balsley

Checkerboard
Library

An Imprint of Abdo Publishing
abdopublishing.com

ABDOPUBLISHING.COM

Published by Abdo Publishing, a division of ABDO, PO Box 398166, Minneapolis, Minnesota 55439. Copyright © 2019 by Abdo Consulting Group, Inc. International copyrights reserved in all countries. No part of this book may be reproduced in any form without written permission from the publisher. Checkerboard Library™ is a trademark and logo of Abdo Publishing.

Printed in the United States of America, North Mankato, Minnesota
052018
092018

THIS BOOK CONTAINS
RECYCLED MATERIALS

Design: Kelly Doudna, Mighty Media, Inc.
Production: Mighty Media, Inc.
Editor: Liz Salzmann
Cover Photographs: iStockphoto (left), Shutterstock (right)
Interior Photographs: AP Images, pp. 25, 27; Clem Rutter/Wikimedia Commons, pp. 9, 28 (top); CoderDojo Foundation/Flickr, p. 23; iStockphoto, p. 7; ITU Pictures/Flickr, pp. 18, 29 (bottom); Joi Ito/Flickr, pp. 15, 29 (top); Michael Hicks/Wikimedia Commons, p. 17; Shutterstock, pp. 4, 21, 24; Wikimedia Commons, pp. 11, 13, 28 (bottom)

Library of Congress Control Number: 2017961602

Publisher's Cataloging-in-Publication Data
Names: Balsley, Christine E., author.
Title: Master computer programmers / by Christine E. Balsley.
Description: Minneapolis, Minnesota : Abdo Publishing, 2019. | Series: It's a digital
    world! | Includes online resources and index.
Identifiers: ISBN 9781532115356 (lib.bdg.) | ISBN 9781532156076 (ebook)
Subjects: LCSH: Computer programmers--Juvenile literature. | Computer software--
    Development--Juvenile literature. | Software engineering--Juvenile literature. |
    Occupations--Careers--Jobs--Juvenile literature.
Classification: DDC 005.1023--dc23

CONTENTS

Daily Computing 5

Computer Communication 6

The First Computers 8

Early Computer Languages .12

A Game Changer 14

Bringing Computers Home .16

The World Wide Web 18

Computer Languages Today 20

Learning to Program 22

The Future of Programming 26

Timeline 28

Glossary 30

Online Resources 31

Index 32

DAILY COMPUTING

It's early morning. The alarm on your smartphone wakes you up with your favorite ringtone. At school, your teacher calls you up to the Smartboard to solve a math problem. After school, you work on a report through Google Docs. Then the doorbell rings. The pizza your parents ordered **online** has arrived! You settle in with your family to watch your favorite show on AppleTV.

All of these activities are made possible by computer programmers! Smartphones, laptops, cars, some **appliances**, and more have computers in them. It's hard to think of any job or product that doesn't require a computer. And every computer needs **software** created by computer programmers. Without programmers, computers would not work and many of the tasks you do every day wouldn't be possible.

CHAPTER 1

COMPUTER COMMUNICATION

Computers need instructions to work. But how does a computer get instructions? Programmers write instructions using languages that the computer and programmer both understand. Common computer languages used today include C++ and Java. The instructions that these languages produce are made up of symbols, numbers, and letters. It can seem like a secret code. In fact, programming is also called **coding**.

Computer programmers work with clients to figure out what the clients need the computer program to do. Programmers need to plan how to reach the desired result. Sometimes computer programmers use a flowchart or sketch to help them plan. A flowchart is similar to a map. It helps a programmer navigate to see how the program will work from start to finish. In this way, programming is like solving a puzzle.

Computer programmers build **software** to do different tasks. Programmers combine the computer instruction code and add

Computer programmers usually have college degrees in computer science, math, or information systems. Many programmers get training in certain programming languages as well.

graphics, video, or sounds. This creates **software** packages that meet the needs of the projects. Programmers often enjoy math and solving **complicated** puzzles. Writing **code** can be fun, like writing a poem or a song. Programming also requires a creative mind. It tends to attract people who enjoy art and music.

CHAPTER 2
THE FIRST COMPUTERS

The history of computing began before electric power was available. The first programmable machine was invented in France in the early 1800s. It was a loom invented by Joseph Marie Jacquard.

Weavers used wooden cards with holes punched in them to give instructions to Jacquard looms. The cards were placed in the loom. The holes then allowed thread to go through to create **complicated** patterns for rugs, blankets, and wall hangings. Different cards could be used to create different patterns. These wooden punch cards did pretty much what today's computer programs do. They told a machine what to do.

The next step in computing was the **Analytical** Engine. British inventor Charles Babbage started working on it in the 1830s. The Analytical Engine

DIGITAL BIT

Before Mark I, the US military hired mathematicians to solve complicated math problems. These people were called "computers."

was a machine designed to solve **complicated** math problems. Babbage shared his idea with other inventors, mathematicians, and engineers.

In 1842, an Italian engineer wrote an article about Babbage's machine. Over the next year, mathematician Ada Lovelace translated the article into English. Lovelace was Babbage's friend and knew a lot about the **Analytical** Engine.

Lovelace used this knowledge to add notes to the end of the article. Her notes included instructions that would tell the machine to calculate a set of **Bernoulli numbers**. Although the Analytical Engine was never completed, Lovelace's work made her the first programmer of a computing machine.

The Hollerith Tabulating Machine was the next invention leading to the computer. American Herman Hollerith invented it in 1889. Hollerith's machine used a similar method to the Jacquard Loom. It read cards with holes punched in them. But the cards were made of thick paper, not wood.

The US government used the Hollerith Tabulating Machine for the 1890 **census**. Each card had holes that corresponded to information about a person, such as their age and where they lived. The cards were fed into the machine. The machine read where the holes in the cards were and recorded the information in a database.

Before the Hollerith Tabulating Machine, people had to record all of this information by hand. Experts believe recording the 1890 census by hand would have taken 13 years. With the Hollerith Tabulating Machine, it only took two years.

After the census, Hollerith started the Tabulating Machine Company. It built and sold machines that could count and record all sorts of information. These machines were used by railroads, departments stores, power companies, and more.

In 1911, four companies including the Tabulating Machine Company **merged** to form the Computing-Tabulating-Recording

Company. In 1924, the name changed to International Business Machines. Today, it is computer company IBM. It remains a leader in computer and **software** development.

In the late 1930s and early 1940s, IBM and Harvard University professor Howard Aiken invented the Mark I. This machine could be programmed to solve **complicated** math problems. Mark I instructions and programs used punched paper tape as well as paper cards. The US Navy used the Mark I during World War II. The machine calculated the best way to aim bombs.

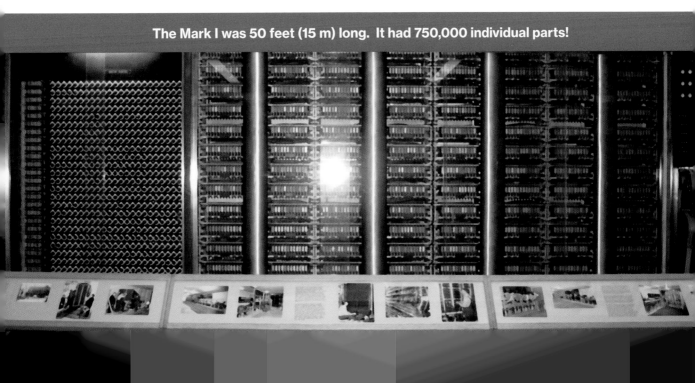

The Mark I was 50 feet (15 m) long. It had 750,000 individual parts!

CHAPTER 3
EARLY COMPUTER LANGUAGES

Grace Hopper was one of the programmers of Mark I.
She was a pioneer in driving computer languages forward.
Admiral Hopper invented the first compiler. A compiler converts
the language of a program from one that humans and computers
understand into one that only computers understand.

Hopper's compiler was called A-0. It converted a
human-readable mathematical language into a computer-readable
machine language. Machine language uses numbers to tell a
computer what to do. Because computers can work with numbers
very quickly, machine language **software** programs are very
fast!

Admiral Hopper's compiler made programming faster
and paved the way to develop new programming languages.
However, the computing world did not accept Hopper's idea
right away. Machine language was still tricky to learn and
took a long time to write. It was also easy to make mistakes.

Hopper was the first woman to receive the National Medal of Technology and Innovation. She also received the Presidential Medal of Freedom in 2016.

In 1957, programmers at IBM released an important new computer language. They named it FORTRAN. This was short for "**Formula** Translation."

FORTRAN uses commands written in natural language and mathematical formulas that humans can understand. For example, in FORTRAN, a programmer could just write "add" to tell the computer to add. There was no need to remember what the machine **code** was. This made computer programming much easier to learn.

FORTRAN opened up all sorts of possibilities for computers! With this new language, computer scientists accepted the idea that a computer could do more than arithmetic. Soon, computers were used to perform calculations in many different scientific and engineering fields.

CHAPTER 4
A GAME CHANGER

In the 1950s and 1960s, computers were known for completing work-related tasks. This included bank **transactions**, organizing business records, and calculating scientific **formulas**. In 1961, programmer Steve Russell changed how people saw computers. He programmed one of the first computer games. It was called Spacewar! Russell's game showed that a computer could be fun as well as useful.

From the 1970s to the 1990s, many video game designers used programming skills to create advanced video games. New programming languages such as Pascal, Delphi, and C made actions smoother and improved **graphics**. Computers now also had more memory. This meant that computer programmers could include

DIGITAL BIT

Russell got the inspiration for Spacewar! from the space race between the United States and the Soviet Union. In the game, two spaceships shoot at one another while orbiting a central star.

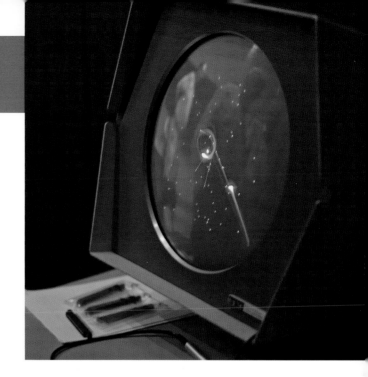

characters and stories in video games.

One of the first such games was Donkey Kong. This game introduced popular video game character Mario. In the game, Mario must get past obstacles to rescue his girlfriend. She has been kidnapped by an ape named Donkey Kong. Mario was later featured in his own video game series, Super Mario Bros.

When these early video games were being developed, computers were still pretty big. And most people didn't have computers in their homes. So, video game **arcades** offering many different games opened up across the country. Before home computers and game consoles existed, arcades were the only places most people could play video games.

CHAPTER 5
BRINGING COMPUTERS HOME

In addition to computer games, other types of programs started being developed. These included word processors and other general-use applications. Knowledge of computer languages wasn't necessary to use these new **software** programs. Anyone could use a computer to perform tasks such as writing letters or school reports.

In the 1970s, computers started becoming less expensive and easier to use. People wanted to have computers at home for personal use. In 1974, computer company MITS invented the Altair computer. It was called a microcomputer. The Altair came in a kit. Users had to build the computers themselves.

When the Altair computer was released, Bill Gates was studying computer programming at Harvard University in Massachusetts. He and his friend Paul Allen used a computer language called BASIC to create a program for the Altair. BASIC, short for Beginner's All-Purpose Symbolic Instruction **Code**, had

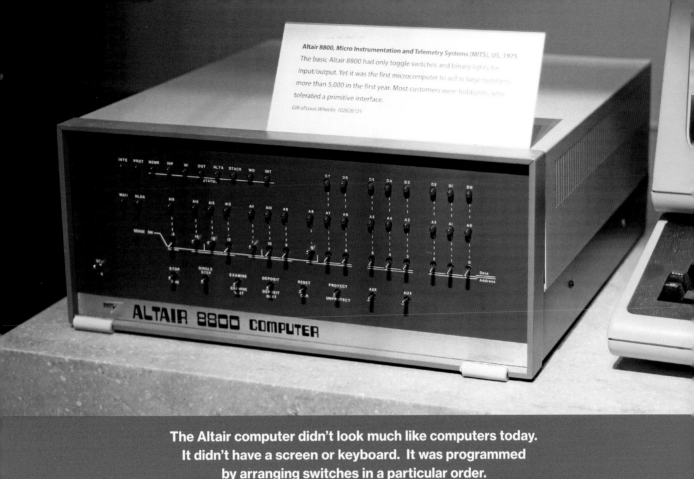

The Altair computer didn't look much like computers today.
It didn't have a screen or keyboard. It was programmed
by arranging switches in a particular order.

been created in the mid-1960s. It was supposed to be easy to learn and use.

Gates and Allen later started the computer company Microsoft. They helped develop the Windows operating system (OS). Windows is now the most used computer OS in the world!

CHAPTER 6
THE WORLD WIDE WEB

From 1989 to 1990, British computer scientist Tim Berners-Lee created several important computer advancements. One was **Hypertext** Transfer Protocol (HTTP). HTTP allowed computers to computers to retrieve links and files over the internet.

Berners-Lee then created a way for computers to assign addresses to the HTTP messages sent between them. These addresses are Universal Resource Identifiers (URIs). He also created Uniform Resource Locators (URLs). These allow computer users to find and connect URIs.

Tim Berners-Lee has won many technology awards. He was also knighted by Queen Elizabeth II in 2004.

Berners-Lee also created **Hypertext** Markup Language, or HTML. This language determines how information will look on a computer screen. With these **technologies** in place, Berners-Lee launched the World Wide Web, or the web.

Berners-Lee successfully created and connected to the first web page in December 1990. But it took a while for word of this new development to spread. It wasn't until 1993 that the web gained public notice and use.

The web makes information **available** to anyone. People around the world can use sites such as Google and Yahoo to search that information. Berners-Lee wanted everyone to be able to use the web. He worked hard to make sure it was a free service that as many people as possible could use. With this new way to use computers came a greater need for more computer languages!

WEB OR INTERNET?

What's the difference between the web and the internet? The internet is a series of interconnected **networks**. Your phone is on a network. So is your computer. The web is pages of information on these networks. The web connects web pages so people all over the world can share information!

CHAPTER 7
COMPUTER LANGUAGES TODAY

With the World Wide Web came blogs, websites, and social media. Users wanted their sites to have more information and to do more creative things. This led to improvements to existing computer languages and the creation of new computer languages.

One of the most important computer languages is C. C has been around since 1972. It is the main language used to build **software** such as the Windows OS and programs that run on it. Many other computer languages spun off of C.

C++ is one of these spin-off languages. C++ lets programmers reuse small parts of computer **code**. These parts are called objects. Because of this, C++ is called an object-oriented language. C++ is used in computer games and web **browsers** such as Google Chrome.

Java built on and improved C++. Java is used primarily for internet programs. JavaScript is a spin-off of Java. It was created

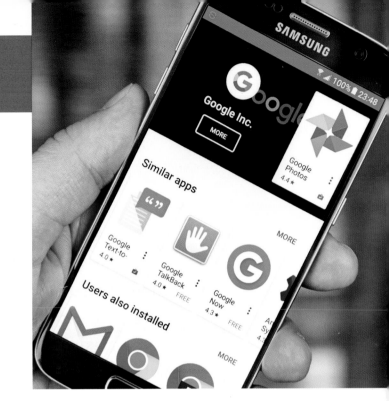

in 1995 to make websites more interactive. JavaScript can be used for Gmail, Adobe Photoshop, and Firefox.

The language Python was created in 1991 by Guido van Rossum. He wanted a language that was fun to use and would encourage more people to pursue programming. In fact, Python is often the first language that computer programmers learn. Python can be used to write scientific and numerical **software**. It is also used by Google, Yahoo, and Spotify.

It is important for programmers to keep up with the latest developments. There are more and more languages created every year. This means there is always something new for programmers to learn!

CHAPTER 8

LEARNING TO PROGRAM

There are more than 15 million computer programmers in the world! And every day there are more and more computers and other devices that need to be programmed. Computer programming is being taught to younger and younger people. This will help make sure there are enough computer programmers in the future.

Several programs teach kids to learn how to program. One of these is Scratch. This **online** program teaches people how to program games, stories, and cartoons. Then the programmers can share their creations on **social media**!

Clubs called CoderDojos offer free computer programming classes for kids starting at age seven. Members of these clubs learn skills to program games, apps, and websites. CoderDojos can be found all over the world.

There are even devices made specifically to help new programmers! Raspberry Pi is a small computer made to teach

There are more than 1,600 CoderDojos in 75 countries!

The Raspberry Pi computer is the size of a credit card. More than 14 million Raspberry Pis have been sold!

programming. It allows users to program and then run experimental programs. In 2015, British astronaut Tim Peake took two Raspberry Pis with him into space. The devices were called Astro Pis. Kids had programmed different experiments for the computers to run in space.

Kids as young as six are being introduced to programming! A company called Wonder Workshop makes products to teach kids about programming and **robotics**. It has robots that kids can program with apps. The apps let kids use music, drawing, or other play activities to program their robots. These products teach programming through music and drawing.

Games are also used to teach computer programming. The computer game Minecraft has a program called **Code** Builder. It teaches kids to program **software**. In Code Builder, kids use computer code to control a robot on screen.

Although more and more people are learning programming today, female programmers are less common. Only 17 percent of people working in computer science are women. That's less than one out of every five computer scientists. But now, thanks to special organizations, more girls are learning computer science and programming than ever!

The program Girls Who **Code** started in New York City in 2012 with 20 girls. Since then, more than 40,000 girls have attended its programs! Girls Who Code offers after-school and summer programs for girls in sixth through twelfth grade. These programs teach the basics of computer programming through fun activities. Projects include building websites, robots, and more.

Other countries are hoping to get more girls interested in programming too. The program Rails Girls offers free weekend sessions to teach girls basic computer programming. Its first event took place in Finland in 2010.

In December 2014, two Girls Who Code students from Erie, Colorado, won Samsung computers for an app they designed and coded.

CHAPTER 9

THE FUTURE OF PROGRAMMING

The field of computer programming is constantly growing! Since **technology** is always changing, programmers are needed to figure out new ways to make ideas happen. There are a lot of possibilities for the future of programming!

One possibility artificial intelligence. This is giving computers the ability to seem like they have human intelligence. Artificial intelligence ranges from face recognition in photos to smart **drones** to self-driving cars.

Improving the security of computer systems, **networks**, and data is also very important. More and more personal information, such as medical and financial records, is being stored **online**. This means more computer programs will need to be developed to keep this information safe and private.

By the year 2020, there will be 1.4 million jobs **available** in fields related to computer science! Who knows what sort of programs will exist in the future? But there will be a need

The company Waymo is developing self-driving cars. In October 2017, Waymo cars began driving on public roads without any human help.

for creative thinkers who like to solve puzzles. There are more opportunities than ever to learn how to program and more fun ways to learn! Could you be the future of programming?

TIMELINE

Early 1800s
The Jacquard loom is invented.

1889
Herman Hollerith invents the Hollerith Tabulating Machine.

1842-1843
Ada Lovelace translates an Italian article about Babbage's Analytical Engine. She adds her own notes, including the first computing instructions.

1930s-1940s
The Mark I is invented.

1957
The computer language FORTRAN is released.

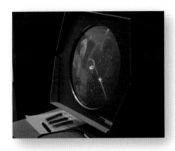

1961
Steve Russell creates Spacewar!

1995
JavaScript is released.

1974
MITS releases the Altair microcomputer.

1989–1990
Tim Berners-Lee develops HTTP, URIs, URLs, and HTML and launches the World Wide Web.

2012
The program Girls Who Code is established in New York City.

GLOSSARY

analytical–in mathematics, able to be solved using the methods of algebra and calculus.

appliance–a household or office device operated by gas or electric current. Common kitchen appliances include stoves, refrigerators, and dishwashers.

arcade–an amusement center where people play coin-operated games.

available–able to be had or used.

Bernoulli numbers–a series of numbers that are calculated by a mathematical formula developed by Jakob Bernoulli.

blog–a website that tells about someone's personal opinions, activities, and experiences.

browser–a computer program that is used to find and look at information on the Internet.

census–a count of the population of a certain area.

code–a set of instructions for a computer. Writing code is called coding.

complicated–having elaborately combined parts.

drone–an aircraft or ship that is controlled by radio signals.

formula–something expressed in symbols, such as a general fact or rule or the makeup of a chemical substance.

graphics–pictures or images on the screen of a computer, smartphone, or other device.

hypertext–a computer system that allows users to access information connected to what is on screen.

merge–to combine or blend, such as when two or more companies combine into one business.

network–a system of computers connected by communications lines.

online–connected to the internet.

robotics–technology that is used to design, build, and operate robots.

social media–forms of electronic communication that allow people to create online communities to share information, ideas, and messages. Facebook, Instagram, and Snapchat are examples of social media.

software–the written programs used to operate a computer.

technology (tehk-NAH-luh-jee)–machinery and equipment developed for practical purposes using scientific principles and engineering.

transaction–an exchange of goods, services, or funds. When related to banking, this includes deposits and withdrawals.

INDEX

A-0 compiler, 12
Adobe Photoshop, 21
Aiken, Howard, 11
Allen, Paul, 16, 17
Altair, 16
Analytical Engine, 8, 9
AppleTV, 5
artificial intelligence, 26
Astro Pis, 24

Babbage, Charles, 8, 9
Berners-Lee, Tim, 18, 19
Bernoulli numbers, 9

census, US, 10
Code Builder, 24
CoderDojo, 22
computer languages, 6,
    12, 13, 16, 17, 18, 19,
    20, 21
Computing-Tabulating-
    Recording Company,
    10, 11

education, 5, 22, 24, 25

Firefox, 21

games, 14, 15, 16, 20,
    22, 24
Gates, Bill, 16, 17
Girls Who Code, 25
Gmail, 21
Google Chrome, 5, 19,
    20, 21

Harvard University, 11,
    16
Hollerith, Herman, 10
Hollerith Tabulating
    Machine, 10
Hopper, Grace, 12

IBM, 11, 13
internet, 5, 18, 22, 26

Jacquard, Joseph Marie,
    8
Jacquard loom, 8, 10

Lovelace, Ada, 9

machine language, 12
Mark I, 11, 12
Microsoft, 17
MITS, 16

object-oriented
    languages, 20
operating systems, 17,
    20

Peake, Tim, 24
planning, 6
punch cards, 8, 10, 11

Rails Girls, 25
Raspberry Pi, 22, 24
Russell, Steve, 14

Scratch, 22
Spotify, 21

URIs, 18
URLs, 18
US Navy, 11

van Rossum, Guido, 21

websites, 19, 20, 21, 25
Windows, 17, 20
Wonder Workshop, 24
World War II, 11
World Wide Web, 19, 20

Yahoo, 19, 21